The Griffin Poetry Prize Anthology

The Griffin poetry prize
anthology

PAST WINNERS
OF THE GRIFFIN POETRY PRIZE

2001
Anne Carson
Heather McHugh and Nikolai Popov
(translators of Paul Celan)

2002
Christian Bök
Alice Notley

2003
Margaret Avison
Paul Muldoon

((The Griffin Poetry Prize Anthology))

A selection of the 2004 shortlist

Edited by Phyllis Webb

ANANSI

Published in 2004 by
House of Anansi Press Inc.
110 Spadina Avenue, Suite 801
Toronto, ON, M5V 2K4
Tel. 416-363-4343
Fax 416-363-1017
www.anansi.ca

Distributed in Canada by
Publishers Group Canada
250A Carlton Street
Toronto, ON, M5A 2L1
Tel. 416-934-9900
Toll free order numbers:
Tel. 800-663-5714
Fax 800-565-3770

Distributed in the United States by
Independent Publishers Group
814 North Franklin Street
Chicago, IL 60610
Tel. 800-888-4741
Fax 312-337-5985

The Griffin Trust logo used with permission

08 07 06 05 04   1 2 3 4 5

NATIONAL LIBRARY OF CANADA CATALOGUING IN PUBLICATION DATA

The Griffin poetry prize anthology : a selection of the
2004 shortlist / edited by Phyllis Webb.

ISBN 0-88784-699-8

1. English poetry — 21st century.
2. Canadian poetry (English) — 21st century. I. Webb, Phyllis, 1927–

PS8293.1.G74 2004   821'.9208   C2004-902535-X

Cover design: Bill Douglas at The Bang
Text design: Tannice Goddard, Soul Oasis Networking

Canada Council   Conseil des Arts
for the Arts   du Canada

ONTARIO ARTS COUNCIL
CONSEIL DES ARTS DE L'ONTARIO

*We acknowledge for their financial support of our publishing program
the Canada Council for the Arts, the Ontario Arts Council, and the Government of Canada
through the Book Publishing Industry Development Program (BPIDP).*

Printed and bound in Canada

CONTENTS

Louis Simpson: *The Owner of the House: New Collected Poems 1940–2001*

Canadian Finalists

Di Brandt: *Now You Care*

Leslie Greentree: *go-go dancing for Elvis*

Anne Simpson: *Loop*

Achieving a shortlist from the more than 400 books submitted this year to the Griffin Poetry Prize competition by teleconferencing is a peculiar experience. Bill Manhire was in New Zealand, Billy Collins in New York State, and I was in a house perched on a cliff on Salt Spring Island, British Columbia. Our negotiations lacked the subtext of eyes meeting, a hand raised in objection, a shrug, a mouth dropping open at an unexpected nomination — the unspoken deeds and gestures that deliver so much of normal face-to-face communication. At length and over several calls we agreed on the seven books represented here in what I hope is an appetizing selection of poems.

Scott Griffin's determination to bring more readers to poetry through his remarkably generous prize should also make a serious writing life more possible for the winning poets. *Competition, judging,* and *winning* are words one might think or feel inimical to the spirit of poetry and poets. But not so. It does not require a Marxian analysis of an economic system and its cultural values to guess where and how standards of excellence arise. And yet there is a mystery. Those standards are usually in flux: matters of "taste," literary fashions, theoretical stances concerning poetics, political climate, and the music of the spheres all help to determine those standards. I find it somewhat embarrassing that all four international finalists reside in the United States, and yet the decision of the judges was unanimous. (We also chose two Simpsons, unrelated, I believe, to each other or to us.)

On behalf of the jury I would like to thank Ruth Smith for her excellent and friendly management of the business of running the competition. When those books she sent began to arrive on my doorstep (not all 400 plus), I felt a thrill at the realization that so many publishers are still willing to take such risks in publishing poetry — slim volumes and a few fat ones not very likely to turn a profit. Ah, beautiful paradox on which we poets thrive.

Finally, to all the wonderfully gifted poets not on our shortlist, writers who might know what William Cowper meant when he wrote, "There is a pleasure in poetic pains / Which only poets know" (*The Task*, book ii, "The Timepiece"), our gratitude for such abundance, variety, skill, and dedication to this compelling art.

— *Phyllis Webb*
Salt Spring Island, April 2004

The Griffin Poetry Prize Anthology

International Finalists

Suji Kwock Kim

Notes from the Divided Country

Suji Kwock Kim's title *Notes from the Divided Country* refers not only to the Koreas North and South and to all the Americas, but also to the countries of the mind. Travelling between past and present, Kim's powerful fictive imagination creates almost unbearably realistic enactments of war zones once inhabited by her parents, grandparents, and even her great-grandparents. If "death is no remedy for having been born," as she says in "The Tree of Knowledge," then perhaps poetry is: poetry as expiation, history, memory treasure trove. In highly sophisticated verse, with lines long and lean or short and subtle, an exorcism seems to take place through the precision and music of her language. In poems about the couple next door in San Francisco, or the poet on the road to Skye in Scotland, or in the streets of Seoul on the Buddha's birthday, Suji Kwock Kim celebrates being alive and well in the complexities of the present moment.

Generation

0

Once I was nothing: once we were one.

1

In the unborn world we heard the years hurtling past,
whirring like gears in a giant factory—*time time time*—

2

We heard human breathing,
thoughts coming and going like bamboo leaves hissing in wind,
doubts swarming like reconnaissance planes over forests of sleep,
we heard words murmured in love.

3

We felt naked bodies climb each other,
cleaving, cleaving,
as if they could ride each other to a country that can't be named.
We felt bedsprings creak, felt the rough sailcloth of sheets dampen,
felt wet skin hold them together and apart.
What borders did they cross? What more did they want?
Bittersweet the sweat we tasted, the swollen lips we touched, the chafe of
        separate loins:
bittersweet the wine of *one flesh* they drank and drank.

4

They called us over oceans of dream-salt,
their voices *moving over the face of the waters* like searchlights from a
    guardtower.
We hid, and refused to come out.
Their cries followed like police dogs snarling from a leash.
We ran through benzene rain, flew through clouds of jet-fuel.
We swam through hydrogen spume, scudded among stars numberless as
    sands.
We didn't want to be born we didn't want.
Blindly their hands groped for us like dragnets trawling for corpses,
blindly their hands hauled me like grappling hooks from the waves,
the foaming scalps of ghost-children laughing, seaweed-hair dripping,
the driftwood of other children who might have been.
Out of chromosomes and dust,
cells of hope, cells of history,
out of refugees running from mortar shells, immigrants driving to power
    plants in Jersey,
out of meadowsweet and oil, the chaff of unlived lives blowing endlessly,
out of wishes known and unknown they reeled me in.

5

I entered the labyrinth of mother's body.
I wandered through nerve-forests branching in every direction,
towering trees fired by feeling, crackling and smoldering.
I rowed through vein-rivers.
I splashed in lymph-creeks between islands of glands.
I leaped rib to rib, rung to rung on the spine,
I swung from the ropes of entrails.
I played on organs, leaped through a fog of sweet oxygen in the lungs.
I clambered over tectonic plates of the skull, scrambling not to fall
down the chasms between, the mind-mountains where I could see no bottom.
I peered through sockets at the brain brewing in cliffs of bone
like a gigantic volcano, with its magma of memories, magma of tomorrows,
I could have played there forever, watching, wondering at the vast expanses
        inside,
wondering at the great chambers in the heart.
What machine made me move into the womb-cave, made me
a grave of flesh, now the engine of beginning driving forwards,
cells dividing, cells dividing:

now neurons sizzling, dendrites buzzing,
now arteries tunneling tissue like tubes hooked to an IV;
now organs pumping, hammers of hunger and thirst pounding,
now sinews cleaving, tendons lashing meat to bone:
meanwhile my skeleton welding, scalp cementing like mortar,
meanwhile my face soldered on, hardening like a mask of molten steel,
meanwhile my blood churning like a furnace of wanting,
meanwhile my heart ticking like a bomb—*is-was, is-was:*
then cold metal tongs clamped my forehead and temples,

then forceps plucked me from mother's body like fruit torn from a tree:
then I heard a cry of pain—mine? not mine?—
then a scalpel's *snip snip* against the umbilical cord, like razors scraping a
     leather strop:
soon I felt sticky with blood and matted fur, surgical lights blinding,
soon I felt tears burning my skin—*Why are you crying? Why am I?*—
I didn't know who or what I was, only that I was,
each question answered by the echo of my voice alone: I, I, I.

Borderlands
for my grandmother

Crush my eyes, bitter grapes:
wring out the wine of seeing.

We tried to escape across the frozen Yalu, to Ch'ientao or Harbin.
I saw the Japanese soldiers shoot:

I saw men and women from our village blown to hieroglyphs of viscera,
engraving nothing.

River of never.
River the opposite of Lethe,

dividing those who lived from those who were killed:
why did I survive?

I wondered at each body with its separate skin, its separate suffering.
My childhood friend lay on the boot-blackened ice:

I touched his face with disbelief,
I tried to hold his hand but he snatched it away, as if he were ashamed of
        dying,

eye grown large with everything it saw, everyone who disappeared:
pupil of suffering.

Lonely O, blank of an eye
rolled back into its socket,

I was afraid to see you:
last thoughts, last dreams crawling through his skull like worms.

Montage with Neon, Bok Choi, Gasoline,
Lovers & Strangers

None of the streets here has a name,
but if I'm lost
tonight I'm happy to be lost.

Ten million lanterns light the Seoul avenues
for Buddha's Birthday,
ten million red blue green silver gold moons

burning far as the eye can see in every direction
& beyond,
"one for every spirit,"

voltage sizzling socket to socket
as thought does,
firing & firing the soul.

Lashed by wind, flying up like helium balloons
or hanging still
depending on weather,

they turn each road into an earthly River of Heaven
doubling & reversing
the river above,

though not made of much:
colored paper, glue, a few wires,
a constellation of poor facts.

I can't help feeling giddy.
I'm drunk on neon, drunk on air,
drunk on seeing what was made

almost from nothing: if anything's here
it was built
out of ash, out of the skull-rubble of war,

the city rising brick by brick
like a shared dream,
every bridge & pylon & girder & spar a miracle,

when half a century ago
there was nothing
but shrapnel, broken mortar-casings, corpses,

the War Memorial in Itaewon counting
More than 3 Million Dead, or Missing—
still missed by the living, still loved beyond reason,

monument to the fact
no one can hurt you, no one kill you
like your own people.

I'll never understand it.
I wonder about others I see on the sidewalks,
each soul fathomless—

strikers & scabs walking through Kwanghwamoon
or "Gate of Transformation by Light,"
riot police rapping nightsticks against plexiglass shields,

hawkers haggling over cellphones or silk shirts,
shaking dirt from *chamae* & bok choi,
chanting price after price,

fishermen cleaning tubs of cuttlefish & squid,
stripping copper carp,
lifting eels or green turtles dripping from tanks,

vendors setting up *pojangmachas*
to cook charred silkworms, broiled sparrows,
frying sesame leaves & mung-bean pancakes,

hanyak peddlers calling out names of cures
for sickness or love—
crushed bees, snake bile, ground deer antler, chrysanthemum root,

the grocer who calls me "daughter" because I look like her,
for she has long since left home,
bus drivers hurtling past in a blast of diesel-fumes,

dispatchers shouting the names of stations,
lovers so tender with each other
I hold my breath,

men with hair the color of scallion root
playing *paduk*, or Go,
old enough to have stolen overcoats & shoes from corpses,

whose spirits could not be broken,
whose every breath seems to say:
after things turned to their worst, we began again,

but may you never see what we saw,
may you never do what we've done,
may you never remember & may you never forget.

The Couple Next Door

tend their yard every weekend,
when they paint or straighten
the purple fencepickets canting
each other at the edge of their lot,

hammering them down into soil
to stand. How long will they stay
put? My neighbors mend their gate,
hinges rusted to blood-colored dust,

then weave gold party-lights with
orange lobster-nets & blue buoys
along the planks. So much to see
& not see again, each chore undone

before they know it. I love how
faithfully they work their garden
all year, scumbling dried eelgrass
in fall, raking away mulch in spring.

Today the older one, Pat, plants
weeds ripped from a cranberry bog.
Sassafras & pickerel, black locust
& meadowsweet, wild sarsaparilla,

checkerberry, starflower. Will they
take root here? Meanwhile Chris waters
seeds sown months ago. Furrows
of kale, snapbean, scallion break

the surface, greedy for life. Muskrose
& lilac cast their last shadows. Is it
seeing or sun that makes them flicker,
as if they've vanished? They shake

like a letter in someone's hand.
Here come the guys from Whorfs
("Whores") Court, walking their dog
—also in drag—to the dunes.

I miss seeing Disorient Express
(a.k.a. Cheng, out of drag) walk by,
in tulle & sequins the exact shade
of bok choi. He must have survived

things no one can name, to name only
KS, pneumocystis, aplastic anemia.
I remember he walked off his gurney
when the ambulance came, then broke

his nurse's fingers in the hospital
when he tried to change his IV line,
wanting to live without meds. Zovirax,
Ativan, leucovorin? I don't know.

My neighbors pack down the loose dirt.
I'll never know what threads hold
our lives together. They kiss, then fall
on the grass. I should look away but don't.

Skins

Pretend I can't see
the lady in pearls mistaking me
for the kitchen help I could have been, or be.

Pretend I can't see
the busboy still working at seventy
bend over painfully.

Pretend I can't see
the maitre d'
pretending not to see.

"Dare you see a Soul—at the White Heat?"
"Anger: anger's my meat."
"So I did sit and eat."

David Kirby

The Ha-Ha

David Kirby's illusionistic poetics are like a ha-ha, "which is not a joke but a landscape trick . . . used to keep cows at a picturesque distance from the manor house." The formal appearance of this poet's stanzaic patterns — so chaste and well-behaved and structurally deft — support the genial but disruptive spirit of these narrative performances. *Talk, talk, talk* about travel, food, more food, art, architecture, Barbara, more Barbara, mother, nuns, Rotarians, Americans, more Americans, etc., little operas with recitative. *The Ha-Ha* is funny and sad, colloquial and learned, full of wry self-observation and social profundities. The poems are accompanied here and there by photographs of a large cow who is not laughing.

Americans in Italy

As I wait in line to get into Vasari's Corridor,
which stretches from the Palazzo Vecchio to the Pitti Palace
      and along which Cosimo de' Medici could walk without
the bodyguard he employed to keep the thugs of the Albizi
      or the Pazzi families from sticking their knives in him,
I am passed by dozens of my countrymen and -women,
      most of whom are dressed as though they're here
not to look at the Botticellis and the Ghirlandaios
      but to play city-league softball or mow the lawn.

The three things Americans visiting Italy worry about most
are (1) being cheated, (2) being made to eat something
      they don't like, and (3) being cheated in the course
of being made to eat something they don't like.
      To these people, I say: Americans, do not worry.
Italians will not cheat you. Dishonesty requires calculation,
      and Italians are no fonder of calculation than we are.
As for the food, remember that you are in a restaurant,
      for Christ's sake, and therefore it is highly unlikely

that your handsome, attentive waiter will bring you
a bunch of boiled fish heads, much less a bowl of hairspray soup
      or a slice of tobacco pie topped with booger ice cream.
Indeed, you have already been both cheated and made to eat
      bad food in your so-called Italian restaurant in Dearborn
or Terre Haute where the specialty is limp manicotti
      stuffed with cat food and welded to an oversized ashtray
with industrial-strength tomato sauce; therefore be not
      like the scholar in *The Charterhouse of Parma*

who never pays for the smallest trifle without looking up
its price in Mrs. Starke's *Travels*, where it states how much
    an Englishman should pay for a turkey, an apple,
a glass of milk, and so on, but eat, drink, and spend freely,
    for tomorrow you will again be in Grand Rapids or Fort Wayne.
As Cosimo strolled his corridor, he could glance out from time to time
    to see if three or four of the abovementioned Pazzi or Albizi
were gathering to discuss something that almost certainly
    would not have been a surprise birthday party for him.

    Also, he could literally walk on the heads of his subjects!
Ha, ha! And if he didn't enjoy doing that,
    I can think of plenty of people who would, can't you?
Indeed, there is another type of American who not only
    visits Italy but also writes poems about the place in which
we, the readers, are made to feel like ostlers or bootblacks
    or street sweepers on whom they, the lordly, step from
one palace to another, never soiling the hems of their silken gowns
    as they tread unthinkingly on such human cobblestones as we,

    and here I remember what my student Ron Jenkins wrote
about just such a poet who had written just such a poem,
    that is, "As a gay man from desperately poor circumstances,
I get bored—even angry—very easily at the lives
    of literate, affluent, heterosexual bourgeoisie,
especially those with the means to loll around piazzas."
    Ha! Ron, I too hate the fuckers, and I hereby resolve
never to be one. That is, I can't help being literate
    and heterosexual, but I'll never be affluent,

and, try as I may, I've never been able to loll,
either in the personal or the poetic sense, and it is perhaps
        because of this very physical ungainliness that I also like,
as a sort of frame around one's personal world, not only a *corridoio*
        or corridor but also the *chiostro* or cloister
that's found at the heart of every monastery so the holy fathers
        of this or that order will have a place to walk and praise God
for His generosity in giving them not only soft breezes and flowers
        and birdsong but also their own sins to contemplate,

        as well as a *studiolo,* or—well, there's no one-word translation
for this term meaning "phone-booth-sized reading room
        with elaborate wood inlay and other fine appointments
intended to inspire deep philosophical thought
        on the part of a nobleperson, generally a duke,
who repairs there when in need of such rumination."
        Corridoio, chiostro, studiolo: snug spaces,
tiny hidey-holes in a world too big for its own good,
        refuges from the sun or from assassins.

        Why, they are like the shapes of pasta or of little cookies,
some like ears, others like pens or butterflies.
        Mr. Wordsworth said nuns fret not at their narrow cells
nor poets within the confines of their sonnets.
        Though I have to say I was just a tad discomfited
the other day: as I was looking through an iron gate
        at the very pretty Chiostro degli Aranci in the Badia Fiorentina,
a man comes up and stands right behind me—
        as in, not merely close to or near me, but *right behind* me,

his toes touching my heels, his breath warm on my neck.
Now who is this guy, you are asking yourself:
  an associate professor of art history? My alter ego? A rogue monk
like the one in *The Marble Faun*? A German?
  And these, of course, are precisely the same questions
I am asking myself! But when I turn to look at him,
  I see he is a midwesterner, from Dayton or Cleveland, say,
or better yet, from Cincinnati, the only U.S. city
  named for a secret society!

  He is a large, rumpled man
and he smiles at me, though sadly, and I wonder
  if he isn't the kind of guy who, when he gets off work,
dresses up as a clown and goes to cheer up sick kids
  in the hospitals there in the Cincinnati area,
but now he's looking out at the garden with the well
  at its center and he's thinking of his own mortality,
and he knows that, in a few hours,
  the Benedictine monks will be walking around

  this same cloister after dinner and thinking about something
very similar, although in his imagination
  he sees them not as monks but as clowns, big solemn guys
with baggy pants and big orange tufts of hair and bright red noses,
  and they clasp their hands behind their backs
and they look at the ground as they shuffle along,
  their size 30 shoes slapping the terrazzo,
and they're thinking, Life's pretty terrible—
  well, no, not really, not when you think about it.

The Little Sisters of the Sacred Heart

I'm bouncing across the Scottish heath in a rented Morris Minor
            and listening to an interview with Rat Scabies, drummer
of the first punk band, The Damned, and Mr. Scabies,
        who's probably 50 or so and living comfortably on royalties,
is as recalcitrant as ever, as full of despair and self-loathing,

but the interviewer won't have it, and he keeps calling him "Rattie,"
            saying, "Ah, Rattie, it's all a bit of a put-on, isn't it?"
and "Ah, you're just pulling the old leg now, aren't you, Rattie?"
        to which Mr. Scabies keeps saying things like
"We're fooked, ya daft prat. Oh, yeah, absolutely—fooked!"

Funny old Rattie—he believed in nothing, which is something.
            If it weren't for summat, there'd be naught, as they say
in that part of the world. I wonder if his dad wasn't a bit of a bastard,
        didn't drink himself to death, say, as opposed to a dad like mine,
who, though also dead now, was as nice as he could be when he was alive.

A month before, I'd been in Florence and walked by the *casa di cura* where
            my son Will was born 27 years ago, though it's not a hospital
now but a home for the old nuns of Le Suore Minime del Sacra Cuore
        who helped to deliver and bathe and care for him when he was just
a few minutes old, and when I look over the gate, I see three

of these holy sisters sitting in the garden there, and I wave at them,
            and they wave back, and I wonder if they were on duty
when Will was born, these women who have had no sex at all,
        probably not even very much candy, yet who believe in something
that may be nothing, after all, though I love them for giving me my boy.

They're dozing and talking, these mystical brides of Christ,
          and thinking about their Husband, and it looks to me
as though they're having their version of the *sacra conversazione*,
        a favorite subject of Renaissance artists in which people who care
for one another are painted chatting together about noble things,

and I'm wondering if, as I walk by later when the shadows are long,
            their white faces will be like stars against their black habits,
the three of them a constellation about to rise into the vault
      that arches over Tuscany, the fires there now twinkling,
now steadfast in the chambered heart of the sky.

Borges at the Northside Rotary

If in the following pages there is some successful verse or other,
may the reader forgive me the audacity of having written it before him.
    — JORGE LUIS BORGES, *foreword to his first book of poems*

After they go to the podium and turn in their Happy Bucks
    and recite the Pledge of Allegiance
and the Four Truths ("Is it the Truth?
        Is it fair to all concerned? Will it build goodwill
and better friendships? Will it be beneficial
    to all concerned?"), I get up to read my poetry,

and when I'm finished, one Rotarian expresses
    understandable confusion at exactly what it is
I'm doing and wants to know what poetry is, exactly,
    so I tell him that when most nonpoets think
of the word "poetry," they think of "lyric poetry,"
    not "narrative poetry," whereas what I'm doing

is "narrative poetry" of the kind performed
    by, not that I am in any way comparing myself
to them, Homer, Dante, and Milton,
    and he's liking this, he's smiling and nodding,
and when I finish my little speech,
    he shouts, "Thank you, Doctor! Thank you

for educating us!" And for the purposes
    of this poem, he will be known hereafter
as the Nice Rotarian. But now while I was reading,
    there was this other Rotarian who kept talking
all the time, just jacked his jaw right through
    the poet's presentations of some of the finest

vers libre available to today's listening audience,
        and he shall be known hereafter as the Loud Rotarian.
Nice Rotarian, Loud Rotarian: it's kind of like Good Cop,
            Bad Cop or God the Father, Mary the Mother.
Buy Low, Sell High. Win Some, Lose Some.
        Comme Ci, Comme Ça. Half Empty, Half Full.

But in a sense the Loud Rotarian was the honest one;
        he didn't like my poetry and said so—not in so many words,
but in the words he used to his tablemates
        as he spoke of his golf game or theirs
or the weather or the market or, most likely,
        some good deed that he was the spearchucker on,

the poobah, the mucky-muck, the head honcho,
        for one thing I learned very quickly
was that Rotarians are absolutely nuts
            over good deeds and send doctors to Africa
and take handicapped kids on fishing trips
        and just generally either do all sorts of hands-on

projects themselves or else raise a ton of money
        so they can get somebody else to do it for them,
whereas virtually every poet I know, myself included,
            spends his time either trying to get a line right
or else feeling sorry for himself and maybe writing a check
        once a year to the United Way if the United Way's lucky.

The Nice Rotarian was probably just agreeing with me,
        just swapping the geese and fish of his words
with the bright mirrors and pretty beads of mine,
                for how queer it is to be understood by someone
on the subject of anything, given that,
        as Norman O. Brown says, the meaning of things

is not in the things themselves but between them,
        as it surely was that time those kids scared us so bad
in Paris: Barbara and I had got on the wrong train, see,
                and when it stopped, it wasn't at the station
two blocks from our apartment but one
        that was twenty miles outside of the city,

and we looked for someone to tell us how
        to get back, but the trains had pretty much stopped
for the evening, and then out of the dark
                swaggered four Tunisian teenagers,
and as three of them circled us, the fourth
        stepped up and asked the universal ice-breaker,

i.e., Q.: Do you have a cigarette?
        A.: *Non, je ne fume pas.*
Q.: You're not French, are you?
                A.: *Non, je suis américain.* Q.: From New York?
A.: *Non, Florida.* Q.: Miami?
        A.: *Non, une petite ville qui s'appelle Tallahassee*

dans le nord de . . . And here the Tunisian kid
      mimes a quarterback passing and says, *Ah,*
l'université avec la bonne équipe de futbol!
         He was a fan of FSU sports, of all things
so we talked football for a while, and then
      he told us where to go for the last train.

Change one little thing in my life or theirs
      and they or I could have been either the Loud Rotarian
or the Nice one, and so I say to Rotarians everywhere,
         please forgive me,
my brothers, for what I have done to you
      and to myself as well,

for circumstances so influence us
      that it is more an accident
than anything else that you are listening to me
         and not the other way around,
and therefore I beg your forgiveness, my friends,
      if I wrote this poem before you did.

The Ha-Ha, Part II: I Cry My Heart, Antonio

— at Dal Pescatore, Cannetto sull'Oglio, just outside Mantova

It's just as the waiter has brought us
                a single buttery dumpling
        stuffed with pecorino, parmigiano, and ricotta

that arrives *after* the porcini mushrooms
                and the seafood risotto
        and *before* the snapper with tomato and black olives

and the duck in balsamic vinegar reduction
                that I touch my napkin
        to my lips and say, "There are no words to describe this"

and then feel the sting of tears as I remember
                where I'd read these words,
        in that book about the trial of the English pedophile

and child murderer who delighted in recording
                the final moments
        of her victims' lives, the screaming, the promises not to tell,

her own tapes used in evidence against her yet thought so horrific
                by the judge that
        he ordered them played in a sealed courtroom

and then, in the public interest,
                to a single journalist
        who would only say, "There are no words to describe this."

*

And even though the waiter arrives at that moment
          to clear away plates and pour more wine
      and ask if everything is good, if it's all to our satisfaction,

still, Barbara bends close to me and asks if everything's okay,
          says I seem a little upset,
      and I cover by telling her the story that Mark's cousin Antonio

had told me about this prosciutto he'd bought
          and had put in his basement
      for curing so it would turn salty and sweet and delicate all at once,

but something went wrong, and one day
          he went down to check
      on his prosciutto, and it was maggot-ridden and moldy,

and here Antonio shakes his head and looks at me
          with a sad smile and says,
      "I cry my heart, David," and only later do I realize

I've used this story as a ha-ha, which is not a joke but a landscape trick
          from 18th-century England,
      a sunken fence used to keep cows at a picturesque distance

from the manor house so they can be seen grazing on the greensward,
          kept by the ha-ha
      from trampling the lawn and mooing at the guests.

*

Your ha-ha, then, is a structure against your chaos.
        And your story about Antonio's prosciutto
     is thus a structure against your psychological chaos, as the poem

about the meal at Dal Pescatore and the hideously inappropriate memory
        and Antonio's prosciutto and the ha-ha
     is a further structure against further chaos still.

Or not structure, maybe, but process, like a walk.
        There's almost no problem a walk can't solve,
     say the walkers, and surely the same is true about poetry and possibly

doubly true when the poem is about walking, as is Campbell McGrath's
        "Spring Comes to Chicago," in which
     the poet talks about walking around that city with his pregnant wife,

eating pizza in one restaurant and waffles in another and somehow surviving
        the Chicago traffic that many do *not* survive,
     for the same walk that can be our best friend can be our worst enemy
                                    as well—

while it is indisputably good to go out walking, it is equally indisputable
        that we may, in the course of our exercise,
     be struck down or otherwise injured, be we in 20th-century Chicago

or 18th-century Durham, where the ha-ha boom waxed and then waned
        after Lord Lambton tumbled into his,
     climbed out cursing, and had it filled with coal-spoil.

*

When the meal is over, we take a taxi to Piadena and the train
          from there to Mantova,
     past these little towns, each with its own *duomo*, great or small,

that bursts from the pavement like Dante's Mount of Paradise,
          and while none is so beautiful as the dome
     of Santa Maria del Fiore in Florence or so Gothic and spire-studded

as the Milan *duomo* that seems to be armed against the devil's legions
          or as vast as that of St. Peter's in Rome,
     the cathedral big enough to brag of its bigness by outlining

on its floor—plenty of opportunities to stumble there!—the plans
          of the other, lesser cathedrals,
     still, were we to get off the train and walk into one of these little churches,

we'd see it's been built like all the others, its interior looming larger
          than its exterior suggests and its vault
     painted in the manner of the night sky, because night

is the best time to talk to God, for if Satan and his boys are everywhere,
          the rates are cheaper then,
     and so we make our way down the aisle, the dark cut only

by candlelight, and figures shuffle in the shadows, though who they are,
          we'll never know, and our steps are uncertain,
     but over our heads, the sky blazes with promise, and the stars are spinning.

August Kleinzahler

The Strange Hours Travelers Keep

The Strange Hours Travelers Keep is a masterful collection of
work from a poet who inhabits the energies of urban life more
fully than anyone else currently writing. If August Kleinzahler's
poems notice birdsong, they do so by their own account as
"part of a mix — footsteps, traffic, / fountains, shouts." There
is something exhilarating about passages of verse which are so
ferociously on the move, between locations, between forms,
between registers. These poems swagger and swerve and sing,
while their moments of grace are ruthlessly sudden and just as
swiftly abandoned to all the other stuff that is happening in the
universe. Kleinzahler's poems also talk a lot about music, and
they themselves live in the miraculous, conditional way that
music does — finding their harmonies by moving forward.

THE STRANGE HOURS TRAVELERS KEEP

The markets never rest
Always they are somewhere in agitation
Pork bellies, titanium, winter wheat
Electromagnetic ether peppered with photons
Treasure spewing from Unisys A-15 J mainframes
Across the firmament
Soundlessly among the thunderheads and passenger jets
As they make their nightlong journeys
Across the oceans and steppes

Nebulae, incandescent frog spawn of information
Trembling in the claw of Scorpio
Not an instant, then shooting away
Like an enormous cloud of starlings

Garbage scows move slowly down the estuary
The lights of the airport pulse in morning darkness
Food trucks, propane, tortured hearts
The reticent epistemologist parks
Gets out, checks the curb, reparks
Thunder of jets
Peristalsis of great capitals

How pretty in her tartan scarf
Her ruminative frown
Ambiguity and Reason
Locked in a slow, ferocious tango
Of *if not, why not*

THE OLD POET, DYING

He looks eerily young,
what's left of him,
purged, somehow, back into boyhood.
It is difficult not to watch
the movie on TV at the foot of his bed,
40″ color screen,
a jailhouse dolly psychodrama:
truncheons and dirty shower scenes.
I recognize one of the actresses,
now a famous lesbian,
clearly an early B-movie role.
The black nurse says "Oh dear"
during the beatings.
—*TV in this town is crap*, he says.
His voice is very faint.
He leans toward me,
sliding further and further,
until the nurse has to straighten him out,
scolding him gently.
He reaches out for my hand.
The sudden intimacy rattles me.
He is telling a story.
Two, actually,
and at some point they blend together.
There are rivers and trains,
Oxford and a town near Hamburg.
Also, the night train to Milan
and a lovely Italian breakfast.
The river in Oxford—
he can't remember the name;

but the birds and fritillaria in bloom . . .
He remembers the purple flowers
and a plate of gingerbread cookies
set out at one of the colleges.
He gasps to remember those cookies.
How surprised he must have been
by the largesse,
and hungry, too.
—*He's drifting in and out*:
I can hear the nurse
on the phone from the other room.
He has been remembering Europe for me.
Exhausted, he lies quiet for a time.
—*There's nothing better than a good pee*,
he says and begins to fade.
He seems very close to death.
Perhaps in a moment, perhaps a week.
Then awakes.
Every patch of story, no matter how fuddled,
resolves into a drollery.
He will perish, I imagine,
en route to a drollery.

Although his poems,
little kinetic snapshots of trees and light,
so denuded of personality
and delicately made
that irony of any sort
would stand out
like a pile of steaming cow flop

on a parquet floor.
We are in a great metropolis
that rises heroically from the American prairie:
a baronial home,
the finest of neighborhoods,
its broad streets nearly empty
on a Saturday afternoon,
here and there a redbud in bloom.
Even in health,
a man so modest and soft-spoken
as to be invisible
among others, in a room of almost any size.
It was, I think, a kind of hardship.
—*Have you met what's-his-name yet?*
he asks.
        You know who I mean,
the big shot.
           —Yes, I tell him, I *have.*
—You know that poem of his?
Everyone knows that poem
where he's sitting indoors by the fire
and it's snowing outside
and he suddenly feels a snowflake
on his wrist?
He pauses and begins to nod off.
I remember now the name of the river
he was after, the Cherwell,
with its naked dons, The Parson's Pleasure,
There's a fiercesome catfight
on the TV, with blondie catching hell

from the chicana.
He comes round again and turns to me,
leaning close,
    —*Well, of course*, he says,
taking my hand,
his eyes narrowing with malice and delight:
—*That's not going to be just any old snowflake,*
now, is it?

The beauty—
the way the swallows gather around the Duomo
for a few moments at dusk then scatter,
darting away across the Vale
with its checkboard pastels dissolving into smoke
along with the hills beyond.
We saw it that one time from the Maestro's apartments,
through a little oval window above the piazza
while that awful American baritone—what's his name—
was mauling the love duet with Poppea at the end,
and she so wickedly angelic, a Veronese angel . . .
When de Kooning, drunk, crashed into us,
then the lot of us staggering off to that bar
overlooking the Ponte delle Torri
and finally drinking in the dawn outside Vincenzo's.
I remember the violist and cor anglais
enjoying some passion in the doorway.
Didn't they later marry? Perhaps not.
And the mezzo from Winston-Salem—
I won't tell you her name; you'll know it.
She was only a girl then, pretending
to be native, with her Neapolitan accent
and dark looks, that extravagant manner
and big laugh the divas all seem to cultivate.
But then she was only a girl, peeking
to check if her act was really coming off.
These actresses and stage performers are always a trial.
By the time you get them home
and properly unwound, the cockerels and tweety birds
already at it, they either collapse

into tears or fall dead away, shoes still on,
snoring and farting like drunken sailors.
But that night, that night it was the English poet
(now much beloved but in those days known as the *Badger*)
who was after her, her and her friend,
the pianist from Ravenna, the quieter one,
the heart-attack brunette, renowned for her Saint-Saëns.
You'll know her name too, and the recordings
she made later on with the mezzo of the Schubert lieder.
But then they were just kids, figuring it out,
suffering dainty little sips
of that tall awful yellow drink, a favorite here,
meanwhile taking the measure of it all,
as if rehearsing for a more important moment down the road.
The cunning, energy and fortitude of these creatures
almost never fails to horrify and amaze,
especially two thoroughbreds like these.
One might easily hate them for it,
but as well hate some magnificent cat in the tall grass
scanning the savanna for signs of meat.
Anyhow, the *Badger* was on form that night.
You wouldn't know him. He was young then,
really quite presentable, even appealing, I suppose,
with a shock of blond hair
and that pale distracted feral look he chose to wear.
I don't know that I've ever seen a human being drink like that.
I mean now the swollen old cunt could pass for Uncle Bertie
but in those days . . . Anyhow, the *Badger*
was well along into his routine: a few bons mots,
feigned interest, the learned quote and the rest,

then his signature:

—I don't suppose a fuck would be out of the question?
The girls took no notice, giggling between themselves
and the inevitable band of toffs and toff-y rent boys
who gather round these things. Love culture,
the toffs, can't live without it: mother's milk,
penicillin for the syphilitic.
And where would we all be without them: their dinners,
soirees, art openings, their expensive drink;
and whose appalling wives could we so generously appall?
Can't get enough of it, these toffs. Or the wives.
So this particular evening the *Badger* was right on chart,
watching, waiting, picking his spot:

—Ha, ha, listen, I don't suppose . . .
when just then Signore Cor Anglais struggles to his feet,
humongous hard-on like a prow in advance of the rest,
and proceeds to blow a heavenly riff from Bruckner,
one of those alphorn bits the Bavarians so adore.
Well now, this provoked an enormous display
on the part of the toffs, sissies, remittance men,
expats—those orphans, those sorry deracinated ghosts—
the lot of them in the ruins of black tie,
shrieking like 8-year-olds at the circus
when the clown takes a flop, out of their gourds,
full up with helium, *Eeeeeeeeee*—
la vie bohème, right out there on the Corso,
a moment to be savored and regurgitated for years to come,
when the cor anglais decides to pass out,
Signora Viola all over him, beside herself,
like the final scene from—well, you name it—

the toffs, etc., carrying on like they had a ringside seat
at Krakatoa erupting on New Year's Eve;
and then I hear the mezzo—all of us,
everything else falling away, the air rippling with it—
up on her feet, singing the "Adagiati, Poppea,"
that lullaby of foreboding the nurse Arnalta delivers
in Monteverdi's *L'incoronazione*, warning
of the iniquitous union ahead, but sung
with such tenderness, an unearthly sweetness.
The entire street falling silent around us,
and the *Badger* just sitting there like the rest,
hypnotized, but now his face gone slack:
astonishment? epiphany? grief? but clearly shaken
and—unimaginably out of character—about to weep.

CHRISTMAS IN CHINATOWN

They're off doing what they do
and it is pleasant to be here without them
taking up so much room.
They are safely among their own,
in front of their piles of meat, arguing
about cars and their generals,
and, of course, with the TV going all the while.

One reads that the digestive wind passed by cattle
is many times more destructive to the atmosphere
than all of the aerosol cans combined.
How does one measure such a thing?
The world has been coming to an end
for 5,000 years. If not tomorrow,
surely, one day very soon.

Louis Simpson

The Owner of the House: New Collected Poems
1940–2001

Louis Simpson has been enriching the tradition of poetry in English for over sixty years, from his eloquent poems of the Second World War to the later, understated, sometimes dyspeptic tales of contemporary suburban life. He is one of the few poets to have kept the art of narrative, of storytelling, alive in poetry, and yet he has done so without any sacrifice of lyric power: the work in *The Owner of the House* enchants and disenchants in equal measure. These conversations with America, held over many decades, are informed by a melancholy clear-sightedness, a generous, wry sense of humour, and a determination to celebrate the true lives and capacities of ordinary people. If Chekhov were reincarnated as a poet into the world where we happen to live, this is surely what he would sound like.

American Poetry

Whatever it is, it must have
A stomach that can digest
Rubber, coal, uranium, moons, poems.

Like the shark it contains a shoe.
It must swim for miles through the desert
Uttering cries that are almost human.

A Friend of the Family

1

Once upon a time in California
the ignorant married the inane
and they lived happily ever after.

But nowadays in the villas
with swimming pools shaped like a kidney
technicians are beating their wives.
They're accusing each other of mental cruelty.

And the children of those parents
are longing for a rustic community.
They want to get back to the good old days.

Coming toward me . . . a slender
sad girl dressed like a sailor . . .
she says, "Do you have any change?"

One morning when the Mother Superior
was opening another can of furniture polish
Cyd ran for the bus
and came to San Francisco.
Now she drifts from pad to pad. "Hey mister,"
she says, "do you have any change?
I mean, for a hamburger. Really."

2

Let Yevtushenko celebrate the construction
of a hydroelectric dam.
For Russians a dam that works is a miracle.

Why should we celebrate it?
There are lights in the mountain states,
sanatoriums, and the music of Beethoven.

Why should we celebrate the construction
of a better bowling alley?
Let Yevtushenko celebrate it.

A hundred, that's how ancient it is
with us, the rapture of material conquest,

democracy "draining a swamp,
turning the course of a river."

The dynamo howls
but the psyche is still, like an Indian.

And those who are still distending the empire
have vanished beyond our sight.
Far from the sense of hearing
and touch, they are merging
with Asia . . .

expanding the war on nature
and the old know-how to Asia.

Nowadays if we want that kind of excitement—
selling beads and whiskey to Indians,
setting up a feed store,
a market in shoes, tires, machine guns,
material ecstasy, money with hands and feet
stacked up like wooden Indians . . .

we must go out to Asia,
or rocketing outward in space.

3

What are they doing in Russia
these nights for entertainment?

In our desert where gas pumps shine
the women are changing their hair—
bubbles of gold and magenta . . .
and the young men yearning to be off
full speed . . . like Chichikov

in a troika-rocket, plying
the whip, while stars go flying
(Too bad for the off-beat horse!)

These nights when a space-rocket rises
and everyone sighs, "That's Progress!"
I say to myself, "That's Chichikov."
As it is right here on earth—
Osteopaths on Mars,
Actuaries at the Venus-Hilton . . .
Chichikov talking, Chichikov eating,
Chichikov making love.

"Hey Chichikov, where are you going?"

"I'm off to the moon," says Chichikov.

"What will you do when you get there?"

"How do I know?" says Chichikov.

4

Andrei, that fish you caught was my uncle.
He lived in Lutsk, not to be confused
with Lodz which is more famous.

When he was twenty he wrote to Chekhov,
and an answer came—"Come to us."
And there it was, signed "Chekhov."

I can see him getting on the train.
It was going to the great city
where Jews had been forbidden.

He went directly to Chekhov's house.
At the door he saw a crowd . . .
they told him that Chekhov had just died.

So he went back to his village.
Years passed . . . he danced at a wedding
and wept at a funeral.

Then, when Hitler sent for the Jews
he said, "And don't forget Isidor . . .
turn left at the pickle-factory."

Andrei, all my life I've been haunted
by Russia—a plain,
a cold wind from the *shtetl*.

I can hear the wheels of the train.
It is going to Radom,
it is going to Jerusalem.

In the night where candles shine
I have a luminous family . . .
people with their arms round each other
forever.

5

I can see myself getting off the train.
"Say, can you tell me how to get . . ."
To Chekhov's house perhaps?

That's what everyone wants, and yet
Chekhov was just a man . . . with ideas,
it's true. As I said to him once,
where on earth do you meet those people?

Vanya who is long-suffering
and Ivanov who is drunk.
And the man, I forget his name,
who thinks everything is forbidden . . .
that you have to have permission
to run, to shout . . .

And the people who say, "Tell us,
what is it you do exactly to justify your existence?"

These idiots rule the world,
Chekhov knew it, and yet
I think he was happy, on his street.
People live here . . . you'd be amazed.

Numbers and Dust

All day we were training in dust.
At night we returned to barracks
worn out, too tired to say anything.

On weekends we traveled long distances
to Fort Worth, Austin, San Antonio,
looking for excitement, walking up and down
with all the other enlisted men,
trying to pick up a shop girl
or waitress hurrying home.

No luck that way, so we'd split up
and agree to meet back at the depot.

*

Now you're by yourself, on Vine Street
or Magnolia, gazing at sprinklers,
a bicycle lying in the drive.

A curtain moves as you pass . . . some old lady.

Then there are bigger houses, with lawns and gardens:
English Tudor, a French château,
Bauhaus. The rich like to shop around.

*

I am a guest years later
in one of those houses.

Looking through a window
at some trees, I ask their names.
"Flowering judas, golden rain tree,
ceniza . . . that's very Texan."

And the birds picking at berries?
Waxwings. They get drunk, she says.

In the room behind me Isaac Singer
is talking about golems, things like men
created out of numbers and dust.

*

Two rabbis once made a golem
and sent it to Rabbi Zera
who tried to engage it in conversation.
But the golem spoke not a word.
Finally he said, "You must have been made
by the numbers. Return to your dust."

I think I can see one now,
standing by the gate,
in the uniform of an enlisted man.

It stands looking up at me
for a few moments, then turns away
in silence, returning to dust.

The Unwritten Poem

You will never write the poem about Italy.
What Socrates said about love
is true of poetry—where is it?
Not in beautiful faces and distant scenery
but the one who writes and loves.

In your life here, on this street
where the houses from the outside
are all alike, and so are the people.
Inside, the furniture is dreadful—
flock on the walls, and huge color television.

To love and write unrequited
is the poet's fate. Here you'll need
all your ardor and ingenuity.
This is the front and these are the heroes—
a life beginning with "Hi!" and ending with "So long!"

You must rise to the sound of the alarm
and march to catch the 6:20—
watch as they ascend the station platform
and, grasping briefcases, pass beyond your gaze
and hurl themselves into the flames.

White Oxen

A man walks beside them
with a whip that he cracks.
The cart they draw is painted
with Saracens and Crusaders,
fierce eyes and ranks of spears.

They are on the steep road
that goes up the mountain.
Their neat-stepping hoofs
appear to be flickering
in the sun, raising dust.

They are higher than the roofs
on which striped gourds and melons
lie ripening. They move
among the dark green olives
that grow on the rocks.

They dwindle as they climb . . .
vanish around a corner
and reappear walking on the edge
of a precipice. They enter
the region of mist and darkness.

I think I can see them still:
a pair of yoked oxen
the color of ivory
or smoke, with red tassels,
in the gathering dusk.

Canadian Finalists

Di Brandt

Now You Care

Di Brandt manages beautifully the difficult job of producing poems that are socially conscientious without being didactic. She knows that the best poetry rests on the authority of the heart. Thus, she makes her readers care not only through the pleasures of form and crafted language, but also through the risky honesty of her articulations.

from Zone: <le Détroit>

after Stan Douglas

I

Breathing yellow air
here, at the heart of the dream
of the new world,
the bones of old horses and dead Indians
and lush virgin land, dripping with fruit
and the promise of wheat,
overlaid with glass and steel
and the dream of speed:
all these our bodies
crushed to appease
the 400 & 1 gods
of the Superhighway,
NAFTA, we worship you,
hallowed be your name,
here, where we are scattered
like dust or rain in ditches,
the ghosts of passenger pigeons
clouding the silver towered sky,
the future clogged in the arteries
of the potholed city,
Tecumseh, come back to us
from your green grave,
sing us your song of bravery
on the lit bridge over the black river,
splayed with grief over the loss
of its ancient rainbow coloured

fish swollen joy.
Who shall be fisher king
over this poisoned country,
whose borders have become
a mockery,
blowing the world to bits
with cars and cars and trucks and electricity and cars,
who will cover our splintered
bones with earth and blood,
who will sing us back into —

2

See how there's no one going to Windsor,
only everyone coming from?
Maybe they've been evacuated,
maybe there's nuclear war,
maybe when we get there we'll be the only ones.
See all those trucks coming toward us,
why else would there be rush hour on the 401
on a Thursday at nine o'clock in the evening?
I counted 200 trucks and 300 cars
and that's just since London.
See that strange light in the sky over Detroit,
see how dark it is over Windsor?
You know how people keep disappearing,
you know all those babies born with deformities,
you know how organ thieves follow tourists
on the highway and grab them at night
on the motel turnoffs,
you know they're staging those big highway accidents
to increase the number of organ donors?
My brother knew one of the guys paid to do it,
$100,000 for twenty bodies
but only if the livers are good.
See that car that's been following us for the last hour,
see the pink glow of its headlights in the mirror?
That's how you know.
Maybe we should turn around,
maybe we should duck so they can't see us,
maybe it's too late,

maybe we're already dead,
maybe the war is over,
maybe we're the only ones alive.

A modest proposal

This night I am haunted by your stray dogs, Frankie,
of Albert Street, their thin, eager love, abject,

you called it, useful, waving your hand, smiling slightly, over
shrimp cocktail and Chablis, nicely

chilled, their backbones broken, flesh frozen into fear.
Let me confess, dear Francis, your confessions were not

unattractive to me, your wife the psychologist busy
helping every poor sinner and no time for you.

Your shaking hand, your heaving trembling chest.
Your twenty year sacrifice of every tender feeling

in the name of civic love. Your soldier's fortitude.
Your impressive million dollar contract to inject them

with whatever poison you feel like to advance our knowledge of
their pain. Like every poet I can

assure you I have prostituted myself for less, gathering fuel in
vacant lots, so *zu sprechen, Herr Doktor,*

wagging my tail, eagerly, panting for healing in the morning and
vivisection at night, suffering

my sainthood graciously, my bowels domesticated,
my howls unheard in the abandoned hermitage.

from Heart

*

Cat in high heels, that wasn't the real story,
though her pink painted hind feet and silly
shoes did make a flashy impression, prelude,
foreplay to the real event, you were right,
I was right, to interrupt the tape, right there,
where it made the turn into darkness,
sadistic pleasure, to talk about fear instead,
terror, Inquisition inspired torture at knife
point, terrific haunting across continents,
centuries, all those lives on the outer edge
of the human, calling, shaking, singing,
grieving, coaxing, dancing them, fiercely,
in the face of this new scattering, shattering,
unnecessary stupid tragic war, back in

from Heart

*

Don't laugh when I confess every cobalt
coloured little lake along the Trans-Canada
is flooding where I cried for you, hungry
tires eating the pavement from Winnipeg
to Couchiching and Shabbaqua, my body
hurtling through spruce scented air toward
polluted Ontario, my spirit reaching long
arms back across the miles to open prairie,
deer among the aspen of La Barrière Forest,
singers around a fire, your filmmaker's eye,
your poet's tongue, your quicksilver
philosopher's mind, quivering skin, naked
heart, how do you know if you're crazy,
these commuter lives, from exhausting
winters in dirty cities to snatched moments
in paradise, being with you, sunflower
mosquito dragonfly grasshopper ice in
the lungs wish it could last happiness

from Heart

*

after Jeffrey Eugenides

How jealous I was finding your beautiful
morning cock beside me, sister, twin, at fifteen,
carrying your gorgeous difference hidden
beneath girlie skirts all this time, and I the
last to know, no, no, you said, it grew when
my blood and breasts came, no one knows
my secret shame, except Rose Garden Grandma,
who told me in her kitchen at age five, rolling
out sour apple pie dough, I know, I know you,
you're *paeve*, and I didn't know what she meant
until age thirteen, and I feeling only left out
and desirous, O, of the urgent heaviness of
your new maleness and unafraid, though it
frustrated and alarmed you, turned my hungry
woman's body over to cover you, and you
welcomed it, O, that was sweet love we made
that morning, dear twin, you pouring your
urgent flesh into me and my thirsty belly
drinking, drinking, until I knew how to grow
my own, and now walking along the sidewalks
in the electric city I swagger a little, feeling
this sweet naked treasure, do you still have
it too, this masculine softness, this heaviness,
hidden in our jeans

Exhibition notes

The Castle and the Winding Path

Great-great-grandchildren of evicted squatters etching poems
into the flagstones. Leather boots. Spiked green hair. Nails.
Glass. Rope. Composition for ten thousand loudspeakers.

Is It Really You

Sweet pang, a continent away. Harp twang.

The Wooden Gate

Spiders swing from the corners in every room. Bees in the walls.
Rusted enamel pot filled with dirt. Prairie happily reclaims
homestead. Roof caves, bows to rain. *Parade of Wild Geese.*
Chokecherries rain from trees.

Wind Chimes

Ceremonies for our remembered dead, iced funeral cakes on cut
glass plates.

A Thousand Hands

Every brick, every stone, tree, bears witness. Lichen under the
fingernails. But we, are we any different?

The Echo in the Echo

The reappearance of the word which unfolds under the word
which revokes. Ten thousand lit candles around a pool.
Darkness.

Allegory: Blue Satin

The love song of the blue satin bower bird, blue pebbles, blue
satin feathers, twigs stained with wild blueberry juice, to match
her eyes.

Except for you, what beauty?

Lit up from within, ten thousand years of waiting flowering in
their faces, hands, feet. These our children, our wounded, our
beautiful, our singing

The poets reflect on their craft

Some days like pulling teeth, rotten roots.
Staring down the barrel of the gun.
Shooting the town clock.
Forty days in the desert.
Fifty days in the desert, no food and water.
The devil sticking out his tongue.
Electric shock. Thunderbolt.
Heroin. Poison in the veins.
Angels beating their wings on your bared skull.
Who will believe you.
Moon in your hands, transparent, luminous.
Cursed by God.
Cursed by mothers, fathers, brothers, the bloody town hall.
Bereft.
Dogs limping on three paws.
The fourth one sawed off by a car wheel, careening.
The devil making faces.
Long red tongue, goats' horns, trampling the streets of Ptuj,
announcing spring.
Licking licking. Cunt or wound.
Bad gas leaking from stones, earth fissures.
Nettles. Poison ivy. Bee sting.
Rotgut. Fungus on your toes.
Wild strawberries low to the ground, cheating the lawn mower.
A wall waiting for the wrecker's ball.
Clear vodka. Ice.

Leslie Greentree

go-go dancing for Elvis

Leslie Greentree is a conversational poet whose artful task is not afraid to engage any subject head-on. Her unpretentious, sometimes comic, lower-case poems have an irresistible charm. They pull us into the funk and drama of her everyday experience and, further, into the centre of her interior life.

sister from the future

she left for Australia a couple of years ago
with five hundred bucks and a backpack
she picked fruit   drove truck   tended bar
did a stint washing paintbrushes for an artist
eventually posing for him while his wife baked gingersnaps
her gift is that the wife didn't mind
couldn't blame her husband for wanting to sketch
the beautiful sister   was a bit in love herself

she called us Christmas Day
I held the phone between ear and shoulder
as I peeled potatoes and checked the turkey
it was Boxing Day in Melbourne
how Star Trek I said
I was laughing until my husband rolled his eyes
and then I stopped
chopped the potatoes with short hard strokes

I thought how fitting it was
to speak to the beautiful sister from the future
I asked her for an inside tip   tomorrow's lottery numbers
thought maybe I would throw these fucking potatoes
in the garbage or better yet just leave them
on the counter to brown and rot
walk out the door jump on a plane
get the hell out of here

go-go dancing for Elvis

why am I always washing dishes when she calls?
she probably thinks I'm one of those people who never
leaves the house   who watches TV all night and thinks
the stars of their favourite shows are real

I sling the tea towel over my shoulder
while she tells me her latest grand adventure
a six month tour across the United States
go-go dancing for an Elvis impersonator
the young slender Elvis of course

she's flying to San Francisco to learn the right Elvis moves
you have to know the right people she says
to be a go-go dancer for Elvis
the beautiful sister has always known the right people
free trips to everywhere   invitations to movie premieres
I guess that means she's always
known all the moves too

what am I supposed to tell her
that I plan to hang out at Totem Lumber in my spare time
next week after I'm finished scraping all the
shit from my walls that was so deftly
hidden by the dainty rose wallpaper put up by the previous
owner   that I was scared to death the first time I
pulled out the lawnmower and how I felt like I'd scaled a
mountain when the grass ended up basically even
and I didn't electrocute myself

while she's being fitted for her black go-go boots
I'll be going through all the boxes I've been avoiding
photographs and wedding shots that never made it into
the album   the birthday cards I didn't have time to
sort before leaving: *happy birthday Honey thanks for seven*
great years   you make me so happy   I love you

I say I'm fine   ask about the tour   make all those
encouraging envious noises I always make
with the beautiful sister   I hang up the phone and
open a bottle of grenache   I'm not going through
those fucking photographs tomorrow

shades of Linda Lee

my phone is haunted by another shadow
her name is Linda Lee
every day there are calls from collection agencies
Linda owes money everywhere and
has skipped town
leaving me with her details
her phone number that doesn't spell anything

I feel a strange sneaking guilt when they call
as if I might really be Linda Lee
they might somehow prove it
the irrational blush of the good girl
accused of lying
who suddenly doubts her own truth

the second week I say things like
Linda's a tour guide in the
Dominican Republic now
I don't think she's coming back
or
Linda left to work with Greenpeace
she disappeared last fall
a tragic dinghy accident   they were
chained to a Russian whaler

these telephone voices remind me of
my ex-husband   parental somehow
slightly disapproving but
too polite to accuse one of anything
to spell it all out

once and a half

the first time you undressed me you peeled me like a small cold
girl who had fallen in the snow your hands were gentle and soft
you stroked me like a chickadee who had tumbled from a nest
when I reached out and placed my hand on your ribs slid it up
over the bones I felt your heart race strong and hard felt how
that was for me because of me   I splayed my hand my fingers
on your white skin pressed gently then more firmly until my
handprint was embedded red in your white chest my bones
impressed upon your skin   it didn't fade until after our
breathing slowed   your heartbeat slowed

sometimes I fell asleep with head pressed to your chest   your
long arms wrapped around me once and a half listening to your
heart like a puppy to an alarm clock wrapped in a towel   your
breath echoing those steady true thumps with soft puffs of air
blowing wisps of hair across my cheek in a matching steady beat

how like me to look for symbolism   to ruin the meaning that
did exist   making it more than it was when in a smaller world
it might have been acceptable   trust me to make a metaphor
from a simple physical response

being Bogey

ever since you told me *Casablanca* was your favourite movie
I knew you would leave eventually   could see how the appeal
of sacrificing yourself to a higher good would be stronger than
anything I could offer you   how you were one of those men
who had to do what was right and honourable

you be Bogart then   lay yourself at the altar of an old empty
promise   at the feet of the children who will eventually scorn
your sacrifice as weakness spit I hate you when you won't buy
them a car or this season's green Capri pants whenever they
turn those practised pouting eyes on your stricken face

who shall I be then   Deborah Kerr in *An Affair to Remember*
she too must have always secretly known that love could never
conquer all the pissy details of reality   that's why she couldn't
offer him her flawed self   shall I sit here now with a blanket
over my legs pretending I'm not crippled

the worst part is that even though I've been hit by a truck there
is still a part of me that knows this is the best way to make you
love me   if you had stayed eventually I would have driven you
away in tiny increments with my sharp tongue and my clawing
need

now you will pine for me always and I for you   absence and loss
the only guarantees of a great and lasting love   the ideal and
torment of what's lost somehow more real than making supper
washing dishes taking out the garbage   but I'm still crippled
still sitting under this blanket and I'm not as drawn to the
romance of this movie as you

"if I was a gate"

I thought I loved the cordless screwdriver
but this is something else altogether
I hold my shiny new electric drill
listen to its high-pitched whine
it is fairly leaping in my hand
tingling through my arm my shoulder
waking all my bones

I am a surgeon
drilling tidy holes
precise and perfect
I blow off the dust
step back to admire my handiwork
brandish my shrieking drill
step in again

you have to make small notches first
you see, in the cupboard doors
I could pull out
my old battered hammer
use brute force
I prefer to take the bit in hand
push it gently into the soft wood
make the small circular motions
that create the slot it
will slide into naturally
otherwise it jumps around
eager but awkward
until you guide it home

there is that small moment as the drill bit
pauses   seeks   slips in
a second's resistance before it sinks
I feel the wood yield under my
steady singing pressure
the bit bores deeper and deeper
until with a start I feel it
I am through

now this is power
like when a lover leaves and
your fear turns into the sudden
realization that you can do it for yourself
just as well or better
and you don't have to listen to the same
Monty Python story
over and over and over
throughout the course of a long
beery evening either

Darryl showed me what to do in Totem
it felt heavy and alien in my hands
I wanted to throw myself at his feet
beg him to come home with me
drill my first hole

now I'm laughing aloud
fiercely proud of the naked apertures
racing across my kitchen
like a banner
now I'm looking around my house
wondering what else I can plunge this into

I didn't put music on
wanting nothing to interfere with the
insouciant shrieking seduction of my electric drill
the song fragment that loops through my mind:
if I was a gate I'd be swinging

New Orleans

for the first part of Carnival
she sends photographs
glowing from them in her
gold Carnival Ball mask
iridescent plumes floating
above her head
purple feather boa tossed naturally
around her slim shoulders

in the next shot they are on the street
she brighter than Elvis again today
neck draped in beads of
green gold and purple
the official colours of Carnival
she explains
green for faith
gold for power
purple for justice

I know what girls do
to earn their beads
imagine the shouts of drunks
leaning from windows on Bourbon Street
the crowd one laughing drinking organism
calling *show us your tits*
of course she would
it's all part of the fun
no one cares what her tits look like
it's the act itself that earns
approbation and gifts of beads

(although the breasts of
the beautiful sister are
spectacular anyway
of course)

there at Carnival I, too
might allow myself to be
carried away finally
flash my breasts
at strangers for baubles

Anne Simpson

Loop

The twin towers collapsing in New York, a plane spiralling down into the sea, a suicide's fatal leap, even a flying carpet "riding on the wing of darkness," such images of falling recur in Anne Simpson's poetry with disturbing frequency. But, as if to catch the fragments of these scenes of fracture, ellipses, loops, skeins, joinings, and the planets on their rounds also make appearances. Many poems are sequences too long to include here, but the breathtaking demonstration of the "Möbius Strip," which glides across the middle of ten beautiful pages of *Loop*, must be mentioned. And "The Trailer Park" series juxtaposes a mundane world of low-rent lives, family squabbles, and lovemaking against the struggles of the great astronomers who helped domesticate the skies, all subjects further explored through craft and lyric in this promising collection.

The Triumph of Death

These watches. Ticking, still. Each hour is cold:
the rims surround quick voices. Shut in rooms.
Gone. *Tick.* The towers. *Tock.* Of fire. A fold
in air. We're smoke, drifting. A painted doom
where cities burn and ships go down. Death's
dark sky — a grainy docudrama. Time
swings bones on circus wheels. Listen: wind's breath,
a shriek. *Theatrum Mundi.* In their prime,
the living. Leapt. That buckling of the knees.
Then gunshots: plastic bags on fences. Snapping.
Or loose. *Thank you — shop — at.* The lovers see
nothing. He plays a lute. She sings. Clapping —
machines sift through debris for the remains.
A sales receipt, a shoe. The silvery rain.

This is the woman you don't know,
— unnamed, undone —
though you've heard how she turned
for a last look and that
was that. No time
for those twelve chapters
to creative awakening, with accompanying
exercises. Lot kept his head
down. Why is it that a woman can't
give up what's already gone? We all know
what curiosity plus cat equals. This time

God snapped his fingers,
reduced the cities to ash,
along with two of Lot's daughters, sons-in-law,
twins in the polka-dot stroller,
rattles on the rug,
a whatnot full of souvenirs:
the straw donkey from Spain, clay vase
from Mexico with the crack in it. Dishes
still in the sink, phone off the hook
and the voice of the angel
echoing loud in everyone's ears.
Told you so.

After that
who was left
to pick up the pieces? Soon Lot was sleeping
with his younger daughters,
but it was all so dreamlike. Across the plain,

the city kept burning. People made little cries
of distress, flames leapt
from one building
to another. Smoke filled the air.

CARPETS

Night was woven through with what we said,
a Persian rug, patterned with random stars.
We sat on the windowsill of a ruined
farmhouse, all of us quiet after talking.
Weeds lay tangled below, a great square
of something intricate, unknown,
and I thought how it could be caught
by four corners: a carpet lifted
into the dark, undulating up and up.
I might have been pulled into the blue-black,
too high, too far, but something called me

back. Yesterday, kayaking, I recalled it
near a silver stretch where herons gather
at low tide. Just beyond,
water runs deeper, faster, the eel grass
slowly brushed this way and that, farther
down. We'd paddled back the wrong way,
though I liked the shallows and then
the cool green deeps. There, before us, birds
ascended as if drawing something
with them, the sheen of water, a wavering
transparency. We could see the slant
of fields, scattered houses and barns,
orange buoys comically bobbing,
and currents opening to reveal,
lower down, many liquid stairways.

They're searching for what remains of a man and two women.
  You've heard the news:
they found suitcases, pills in bottles, little things that don't matter.
  What everyone wants is their beauty,

now they've taken it. After forty-eight hours it's still unconfirmed, but
  women are already weeping
across the country for the child recalled on television, saluting the flag-
  draped coffin

and taking his mother's black-gloved hand. They knew one day
  he'd resemble
his father, in this hour of the nation, home of the brave. Myths
  have a way of lulling us

with inflatable ease. Anything will do: a beckoning ocean on a sunny day
  in July, idle and devoid
of clues about what might have happened, might have in each thoughtless
  wave. Things wash up

on the sand, described every hour on the hour, so he'll die many times,
  replayed with Greek effect.
(In the motorcade in Dallas, the men were thrust forward, back, almost
  comically,

while a woman in a perfect suit — spattered with blood, bits of flesh — reached
  out her hand for help
as she climbed over the seats.) It's the end of another day; something fades
  into grey, keeps fading, and diminishes.

*

I spent one summer night — too hot to turn over, too hot to sleep — dreaming
    of a plane dipping
over a glassy sea, the sky hazy and suffused with the glow of evening.
    All night

I flew into a lip between air and ocean, an ending without the usual shocks,
    only embrace,
those arms of indolence. This morning they announced the deaths,
    referring to temperature and time —

twelve hours, eighteen — that anyone could survive. But we all knew
    it happened instantly, and then
one body trailed another down, water passing over them, through them
    like combs. One woman's hair, loose

and pretty, fanned around her face as she descended, leaving parties
    under the stars, guests mingling
on a level, grassy lawn, while a pleasure boat drifted in the bay — sails slack —
    leaving a foamless wake.

*

Go back. The final moment comes when the plane, high up, swivels
    upside down, without horizon,
that plausible, straight line, and hangs, hangs — about to descend, spiralling
    crazily — while the mind

clings to its shelf of rattling trinkets. What can't be happening is.
    And is
and is. Until it can't be thought. The doves of rescue fail;
    we take our leave. But remember

that private world of detail. Think of her coming downstairs in the small
    hours, imagine her
in a nightgown, face pale in the light of the fridge. The way he used to sleep
    with his arms flung wide

across the rumpled sheets, duvet on the floor: ordinary lives are always
    embellished by the papers.
Distance magnifies or shrinks — a plane, a toy lost from a pocket — either way,
    something's gone for good.

Whose?

This is a boy's body. Visited, like Sainte-Thérèse, by visions.

On his wrist

are many heads of obscure Chinese scholars, buried to their necks in sand. You might think of the heads as attached to bodies, or sliced from them by a dozen swordsmen.

There are tiny dots to represent the hundred heads. Or perhaps the dots signify the sand, in which the heads have disappeared.

On his left thigh

Alexander's famous phalanx, a box formation (moving hedge of bodies) that saved the Greeks.

Who was it they were fighting?

On his right toe

is a tiny face, but not one any of us know. (It could be a miniature portrait of the nameless woman who lived on the Steppes and rode a horse as well as any man, hunted with falcons, and had six children before she was twenty-four. When her youngest child died, she put two pieces of felt over its eyes, as she had done with five others.)

On his neck

a miniature human body, bird-headed creature from the caves of Lascaux.

Was there ever such a thing?

On his right earlobe

Jumbo the elephant, killed on the railway tracks in St. Thomas, Ontario, in 1885, squeezed between two trains. Its tusks became scimitars piercing its brain, but it did not die right away.

Something remains.

On his left eyelid

a symbol for Planck time that can't be deciphered easily. More beautiful than the Big Bang itself,

this tattoo, and more original.

The body

is that of a boy killed in a convenience store in a small town.

The murderer was a few years older, wearing a death's head mask, carrying a hunting knife.

A tattoo of wounds.

How perfect the flesh, just

before a body is cremated.

History is whatever
lingers.

Di Brandt grew up in Reinland, Manitoba, a Mennonite farming village, and was one of the first women writers to break the public silence of Mennonite women in Canada. Her poetry has been awarded the Gerald Lampert Memorial Award, the McNally Robinson Manitoba Book of the Year Award, and the CAA National Poetry Award. She has been shortlisted twice for the Governor General's Award and has been nominated for the Commonwealth Poetry Prize and the Pat Lowther Memorial Award. Her books include *questions i asked my mother; Agnes in the sky; mother, not mother;* and *Jerusalem, beloved.* She currently teaches Creative Writing and Canadian Literature at the University of Windsor. *Now You Care* was published in 2003 by Coach House Books and has also been shortlisted for the 2004 Trillium Book Award and Pat Lowther Memorial Award.

Leslie Greentree was born in Grande Prairie, Alberta, and earned a Bachelor of Arts (English) and a Bachelor of Education at the University of Lethbridge. As well as working full-time at Red Deer Public Library, she does freelance writing and acts as associate editor of *artichoke*, a Central Alberta cultural tabloid. She recently won the CBC Poetry Face-off for Calgary. Her first book of poetry, *guys named Bill*, was published in 2002 by Frontenac House, and was followed by *go-go dancing for Elvis*, published in 2003 by Frontenac House.

Suji Kwock Kim is a graduate of Yale University and holds a Master of Fine Arts from the Iowa Writers' Workshop. She was a Fulbright Scholar at Seoul National University and a Stegner Fellow at Stanford University. Kim won the 2002 Walt Whitman Award from the Academy of American Poets for *Notes from the Divided Country*, her first book of poetry. She is the recipient of fellowships from the National Endowment for the Arts and the Fine Arts Work Center in Provincetown. Her poems have appeared in *The Nation, The New Republic, Poetry, Yale Review, Harvard Review, Threepenny Review, DoubleTake, Ploughshares,* and *Asian-American Poetry: The Next Generation.* She divides her time between San Francisco and New York. *Notes from the Divided Country* was published in 2003 by Louisiana State University Press.

David Kirby is a graduate of Louisiana State University and received his PhD in English from Johns Hopkins University. He has won the Brittingham Prize in Poetry and his work has appeared in *Best American Poetry 2000* and *2001*, as well as the *Pushcart Prize Anthology*. He has been awarded a Guggenheim Fellowship and grants from the National Endowment for the Arts and Florida Arts Council. Kirby is the author or co-author of twenty-two books, including *The House of Blue Light* and *The Traveling Library*. A member of the National Book Critics Circle, he writes regularly for the *New York Times Book Review*, the *Atlanta Journal-Constitution*, and the *San Francisco Chronicle*. He is Robert O. Lawton Distinguished Professor of English at Florida State University, where he has taught since 1969, and he lives in Tallahassee. *The Ha-Ha* was published in 2003 by Louisiana State University Press.

August Kleinzahler is a native of Jersey City, New Jersey, and is the recipient of an award from the John Simon Guggenheim Foundation, the Lila Acheson Wallace/Reader's Digest Award for Poetry, an Academy Award in Literature from the American Academy of Arts and Letters, and a Berlin Prize Fellowship. He has taught creative writing at Brown University, the University of California at Berkeley, and the Iowa Writers' Workshop, as well as to homeless veterans in the San Francisco Bay Area. His books include *A Calendar of Airs*; *Storm over Hackensack*; *Earthquake Weather*; *Red Sauce, Whiskey and Snow*; and *Green Sees Things in Waves*. His poems have appeared in many publications, including *The New Yorker*, *The American Poetry Review*, *Poetry*, and *The Paris Review*. Kleinzahler lives in San Francisco. *The Strange Hours Travelers Keep* was published in 2003 by Farrar, Straus and Giroux.

Anne Simpson's first collection of poetry, *Light Falls Through You*, won the Gerald Lampert Memorial Award and the Atlantic Poetry Prize and was a finalist for the Pat Lowther Memorial Award. Her first novel, *Canterbury Beach*, was shortlisted for the 2002 Thomas Head Raddall Atlantic Fiction Award. In 1997 her short story "Dreaming Snow" shared the Journey Prize, and in 1999 she was awarded the Bliss Carman Poetry Award. Anne Simpson has lived in Italy, West Africa, and the United Kingdom. Currently she lives with her family in Antigonish, Nova Scotia, where she has worked for seven years as the Coordinator of the Writing Centre at St. Francis Xavier University. *Loop* was published in 2003 by McClelland & Stewart.

Louis Simpson was born in Jamaica. After studying at Columbia University and the University of Paris, he earned his PhD at Columbia, where he went on to teach. He has won the Pulitzer Prize, as well as the 1998 Harold Morton Landon Translation Award from the Academy of American Poets. Among his many other honours are the Prix de Rome, fellowships from the Guggenheim Foundation, and the Columbia Medal for Excellence. He published his first book of poems, *The Arrivistes*, in 1949. His other books of poetry include *A Dream of Governors*; *At the End of the Open Road, Poems*; *Adventures of the Letter I*; *Searching for the Ox*; *Armidale*; *Caviare at the Funeral*; *The Best Hour of the Night*; *In the Room We Share*; *There You Are*; and *Nombres et poussière*. His other published works include several widely acclaimed books of criticism. Louis Simpson lives in Setauket, New York. *The Owner of the House* was published in 2003 by BOA Editions.

ACKNOWLEDGEMENTS

The publisher thanks the following for their kind permission to reprint the work contained in this volume:

"Generation," "Borderlands," "Montage with Neon, Bok Choi, Gasoline, Lovers & Strangers," "The Couple Next Door," and "Skins" from *Notes from the Divided Country* by Suji Kwock Kim are reprinted by permission of Louisiana State University Press.

"Americans in Italy," "The Little Sisters of the Sacred Heart," "Borges at the Northside Rotary," and "The Ha-Ha, Part II: I Cry My Heart, Antonio" from *The Ha-Ha* by David Kirby are reprinted by permission of Louisiana State University Press.

"The Strange Hours Travelers Keep," "The Old Poet, Dying," "A History of Western Music: Chapter 11," and "Christmas in Chinatown" from *The Strange Hours Travelers Keep* by August Kleinzahler are reprinted by permission of Farrar, Straus and Giroux.

"American Poetry," "A Friend of the Family," "Numbers and Dust," "The Unwritten Poem," and "White Oxen" from *The Owner of the House: New Collected Poems 1940–2001* by Louis Simpson are reprinted by permission of BOA Editions, Ltd.

The excerpts "1" and "2" from "Zone: <le Détroit>," "A modest proposal," the excerpts "'Cat in high heels, . . .'," "'Don't laugh when I confess . . .'," and "*after Jeffrey Eugenides*" from "Heart," "Exhibition notes," and "The poets reflect on their craft" from *Now You Care* by Di Brandt are reprinted by permission of Coach House Books.